paper Flowers

Welcome to the world of paper flowers! Jennifer Maker has designed these paper flowers by carefully studying the structure of each flower and selecting readily available craft materials that closely replicate the look and texture of real flowers.

As a bonus, this book includes links to downloadable SVG files for six of the flowers that can be used with a Cricut Maker™ to make cutting faster and easier!

Instructions and supplies given are for making one flower. We also included photos and suggestions for some fabulous projects using multiple flowers. If you wish to make any of these or use your creativity to design your own projects, remember to purchase any additional supplies you may need.

3 .... Anemone

7 .... Chrysanthemum

13 .... Dahlia

17 .... Giant Daisy

21 .... Rose

27 .... Poppy

31 .... Dandelion

35 .... Orchid

39 .... Peony

43 .... Giant Tea Rose

48 .... Meet Jennifer

LEISURE ARTS, INC. • Maumelle, Arkansas

I0883493

Finished Flower Size: approximately 3" diameter

Anemone

Blooming in the spring, the Anemone is sometimes called the "windflower" for the way its cupped blossom dances in the breeze. Anemone colors include shades of blue, purple, white, red, and pink. When making this flower you can either cut out the pieces using a Cricut Maker™ or scissors.

Shopping List

(for 1 flower)

- ☐ 65 lb cardstock (blue, black, and green)
- ☐ green floral tape
- ☐ green cloth-covered 24-gauge stem wire
- ☐ tracing paper (optional)
- ☐ hot glue gun and glue sticks
- ☐ pencil
- ☐ scissors
- ☐ needle-nose pliers
- ☐ Cricut Maker™ (optional)

To make one Anemone:

To use a Cricut Maker to cut, begin with Step 1. To use scissors to cut, begin with Step 2.

1. To download the SVG files for use with the Cricut Maker™ go to: bit.ly/7241_anemone. If you need instructions on how to download SVG files, go to https://jennifermaker.com/paper-flowers-book. Once all the patterns are cut, skip to Step 3.

2. Make photocopies of the petal patterns A-I, sepal, and leaf, page 5. **Note:** If you don't have access to a copier, you can trace the patterns onto tracing paper and cut out. Use the patterns to cut out the number of pieces indicated on each pattern from cardstock.

3. Overlap and glue the base of a petal together at the slit to form a cup shape. Using your fingers, roll the tips of the petal outward. Repeat to make a total of 8 petals.

4. Overlapping the bases by about 1/2", glue 2 petals together opposite each other. Glue 2 more petals behind the first 2 at 90° angles from the first petals. Turn the flower over and working from the bottom, glue the remaining petals around the base at 45° angles to the original 4 petals.

5. Using your fingers, roll the edges of the small center inward. Center and glue the small center to the large center. Glue the centers to the center of the flower.

DIY Project Suggestion:

Fill a shadow box with flower blooms to show off their beauty and protect your paper flowers from dust and humidity. You can make your flowers all the same color, shades of one color, or mix it up with different color blooms. Skip adding the floral wire in Step 6 and just glue the sepal and leaves to the bottom of the flower.

6. Insert the stem through the center of the sepal*; bend the wire tip over 1/4" and glue the bended wire to the sepal. With the wire sandwiched between the sepal and flower, glue the sepal to the bottom of the flower.

7. Glue the leaves to the floral wire under the flower. Starting just below the sepal, wrap the stem and glued ends of the leaves with floral tape.

* If you are planning to use your finished flowers in a shadow box,similar to our DIY Project Suggestion,page 4, omit the stemand glue the sepal and leavesdirectly to the bottom of the flower.

Anemone Patterns

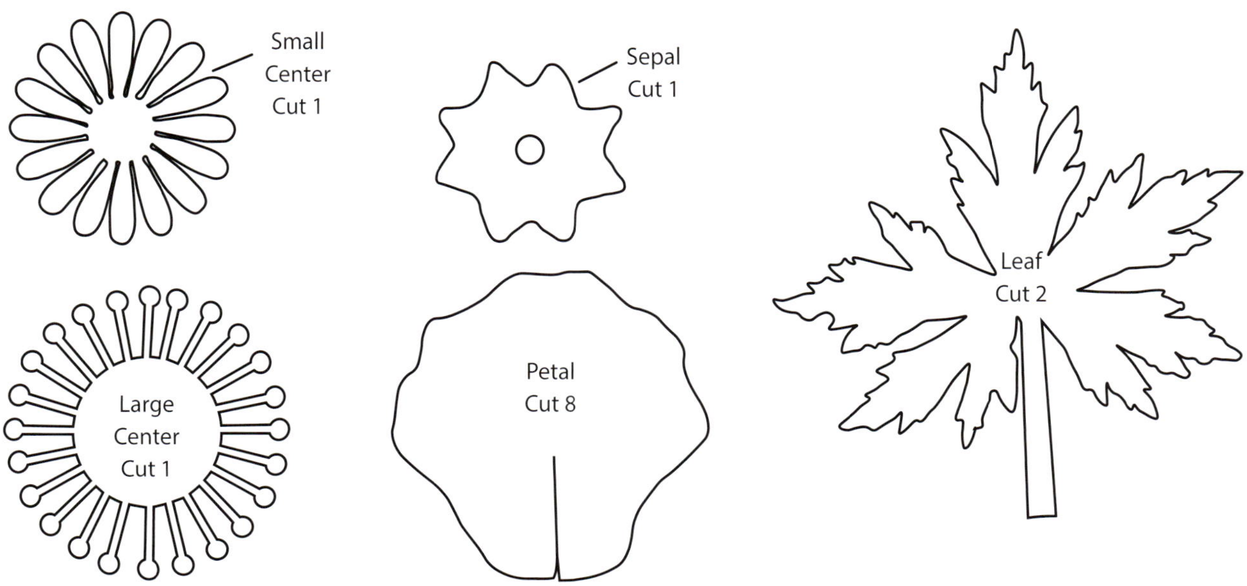

Leisure Arts Inc., grants the owner of this book permission to copy the patterns on this page for personal use only.

Finished Flower Size: approximately $2^1/_2$"diameter

Chrysanthemum

Crepe paper is the secret to making the wispy, delicate petals of the chrysanthemum. More commonly known as "mums", Chrysanthemums come in a variety of colors including shades of red, yellow, pink, magenta, and even blue. When making this flower you can either cut out the pieces using a Cricut Maker™ or scissors.

Shopping List
(for 1 flower)

- ☐ crepe paper (desired flower color and green)
- ☐ green cloth-covered 20-gauge stem wire
- ☐ green floral tape
- ☐ tracing paper
- ☐ craft glue
- ☐ pencil
- ☐ straight pins
- ☐ scissors
- ☐ Cricut Maker™ (optional)

To make one Chrysanthemum:

If using a Cricut Maker, begin with Step 1. If using scissors, begin with Step 2.

1. To download SVG files to use with the Cricut Maker™, go to: bit.ly/7241_chrysanthemum. If you need instructions on how to download SVG files, go to https://jennifermaker.com/paper-flowers-book. Save the scraps. Once all the pieces are cut, skip to Step 3.

2. Make photocopies of the petals A-D, center circle, sepal, and leaf patterns, pages 10-11. **Note:** If you don't have access to a copier, you can trace the patterns onto tracing paper. Cut out patterns A-D on the red lines. Pin A-D and the center circle pattern to the flower crepe paper; cut out on black lines. Pin the sepal and leaf patterns to the green crepe paper; cut out on black lines. Save the scraps.

3. To make the flower center, roll paper scraps into an approximately 1" diameter ball. Insert a stem into the ball and secure with glue. With the wrong side facing up, place a thin line of glue close to the edge of the center circle. Wrap the center circle around the ball and stem, like wrapping a lollipop; securing with more glue and floral tape as needed.

4. Working with one strip at a time, roll the tips of petals A-D around the pencil to slightly curl the tips. When assembling the flower, the tips should always curl toward the center.

5. Place a line of glue along the bottom (straight) edge of one petal A; wrap around the base of the center. Starting 1/2 turn from the end of the first A, glue and wrap the remaining petal A around the base.

6. Place a line of glue along the bottom (straight) edge of one petal B. Starting 1/2 turn from the end of A, wrap petal B around the base of the center. Starting 1/2 turn from the end of the first B, glue and wrap the remaining petal B around the base.

7. Always starting 1/2 turn from the end of the previous petal, repeat Step 5 to add petals C and D.

8. Place a line of glue along the bottom (straight) edge of the sepal; wrap the sepal around the base.

9. Wrap the bottom edge of the sepal with floral tape. Moving down the stem, continue wrapping the floral tape for about 1 1/2" before catching the stem of one leaf in the wraps. Add the second leaf about 1" below the first; continue wrapping with tape for another 1 1/2".

Chrysanthemum Patterns

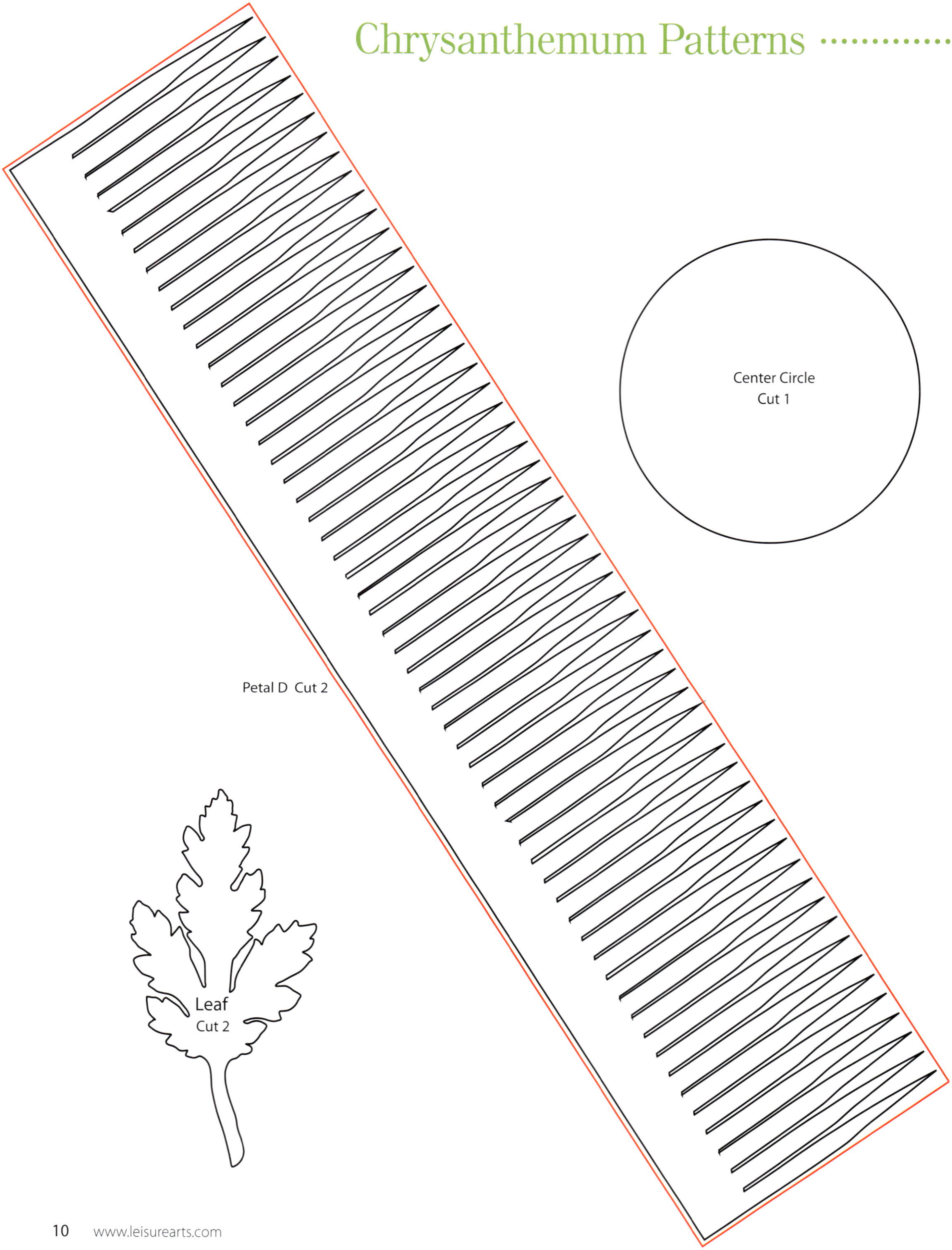

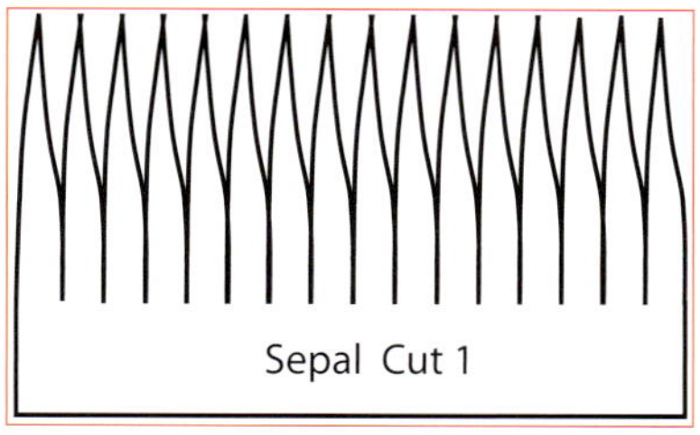

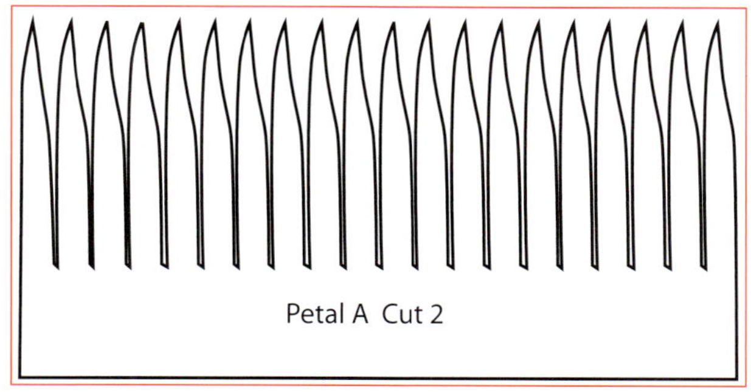

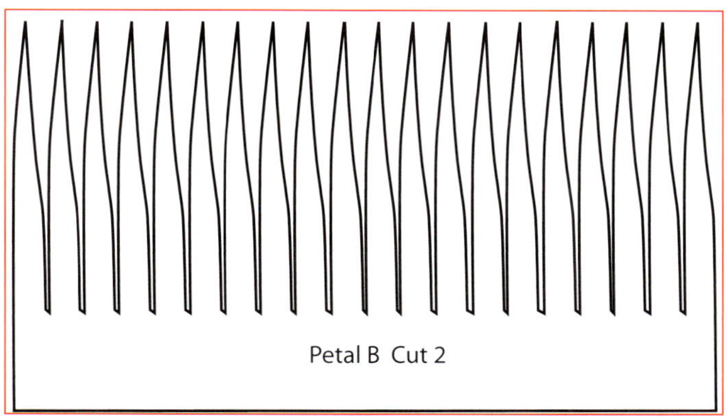

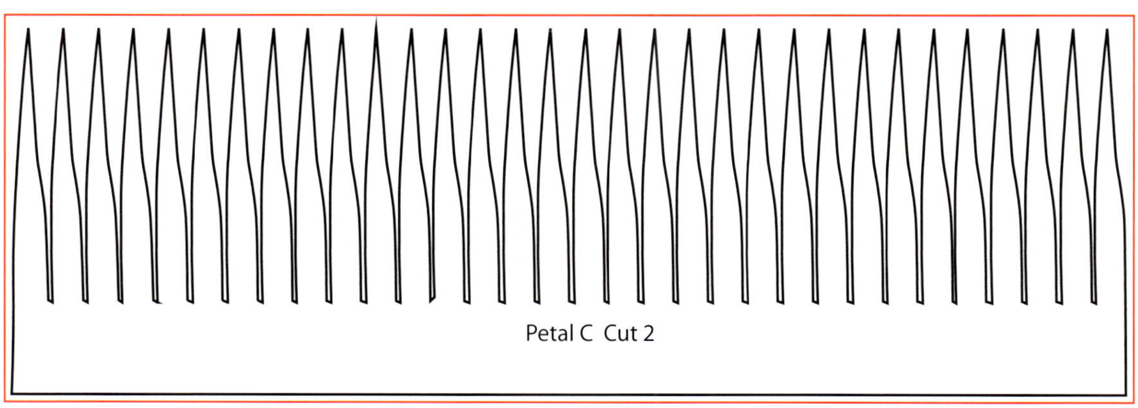

Leisure Arts Inc., grants the owner of this book permission to copy the patterns on pages 10 & 11 for personal use only.

Finished Flower Size: approximately 14" diameter

Dahlia

The Dahlia is a large flower with symmetrically -spaced petals. Dahlias come in many colors including shades of red, pink, white, yellow, green, blue, and purple. Using cardstock for the petals provides stability to help the flower keep its shape. When making this flower you can either cut out the pieces using a Cricut Maker™ or scissors.

Shopping List

(for 1 flower)

- ☐ 12" x 12" sheets of metallic cardstock (1 blue and 6 green)
- ☐ 1 2" x 9" rectangle of metallic cardstock (gold for stamen)
- ☐ 5 1/2" diameter sturdy paper plate or cardboard circle
- ☐ tracing paper (optional)
- ☐ hot glue and glue sticks
- ☐ pencil
- ☐ scissors
- ☐ Cricut Maker™ (optional)

To make one Dahlia:

To use a Cricut Maker to cut, begin with Step 1. To use scissors to cut, begin with Step 2.

1. To download SVG files for use with the Cricut Maker™ go to: bit.ly/7241_dahlia. If you need instructions on how to download SVG files, go to https://jennifermaker.com/paper-flowers-book Once all the patterns are cut, skip to Step 3.

2. Make photocopies of the petals A-E, center, and stamen patterns, pages 14-15. **Note:** If you don't have access to a copier, you can trace the patterns onto tracing paper and cut out. Use the patterns to cut out the number of pieces indicated on each pattern from cardstock.

3. To make petals A-D, overlap the outer tabs of a petal A to the center tab to create a curled petal; glue. Repeat for each petal A-D.

4. Spacing the petals about 3/8" apart with the petal ends about 1" inside the outer edge of the base, glue the A petals around the base. Placing the petal ends about 1/2" closer to the center and alternating the placement between the A petals, glue the B petals around the base. In the same manner, continue to add rounds of C and D petals.

5. To make the center, wrap each center petal around the pencil to curl inward. Apply a thin line of glue along the straight edge of the stamen. Beginning at one short edge, tightly roll the stamen. Fluff and spread the fringed edge of the stamen. Glue the flat end of the stamen to the middle of the center. Glue the center to the middle of the base. **Note:** There will be a small gap between the center and the D petals.

6. Roll and glue the E petals into loose tubes. Glue the tubes between the Center and the D petals, filling in the gap.

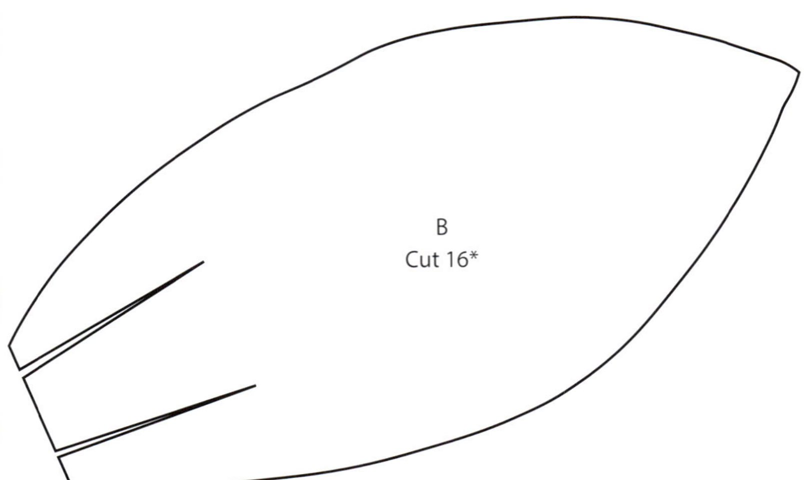

*From your desired combination of blue and green paper, cut a total of 16 of each of each pattern A-E.

Dahlia Patterns

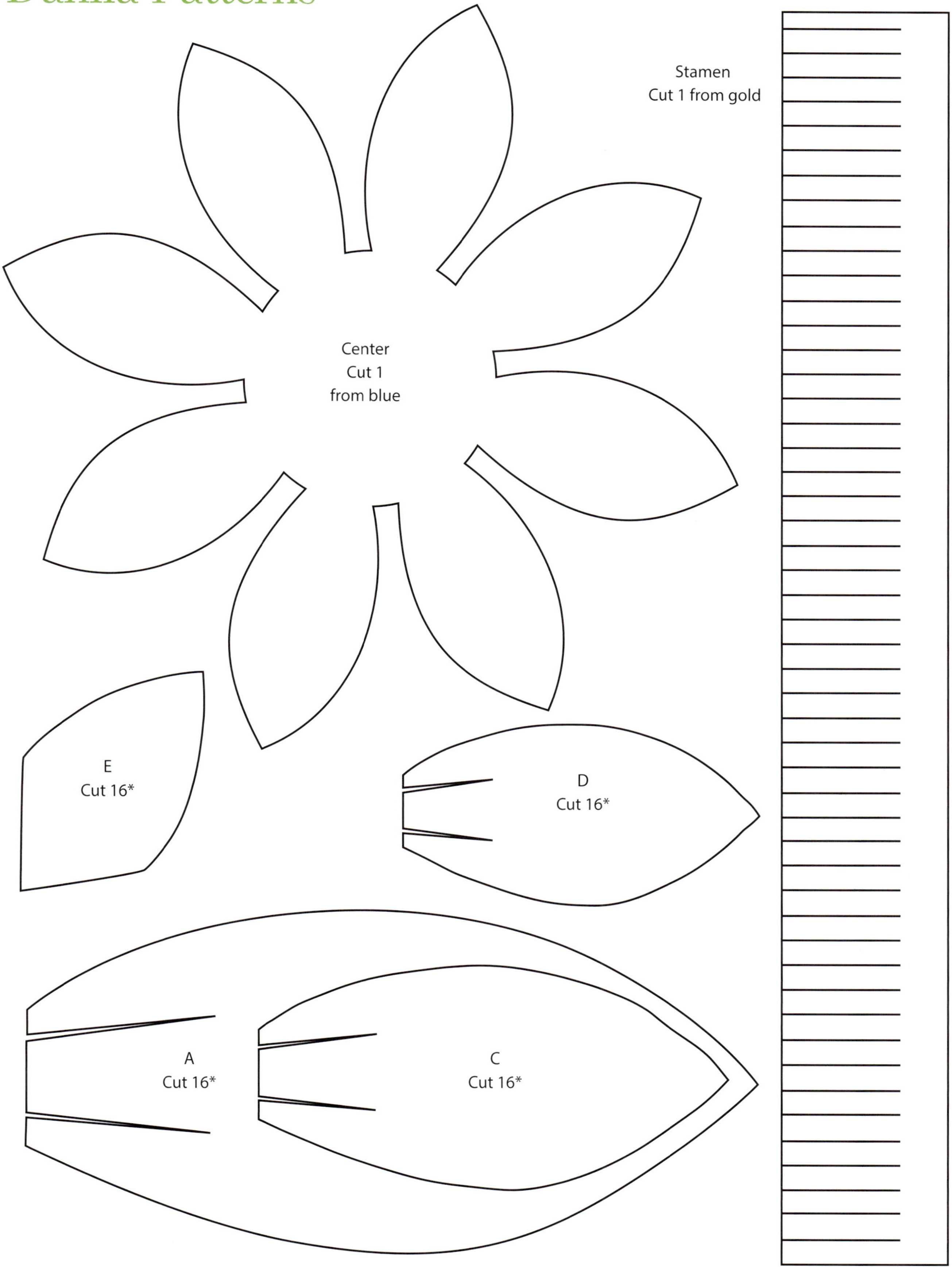

Leisure Arts Inc., grants the owner of this book permission to copy the patterns on this page for personal use only.

Finished Flower Size: approximately 20" diameter

Giant Daisy

Paper plates aren't just for picnics, they also make awesome giant Daisies! These traditional yellow and white daisies were inspired by the Shasta daisy. Other daisy varieties come in shades red, pink, and orange so choose your paper plate colors and have fun making some blooms!

Shopping List

(for 1 flower)

- ☐ 9 9"-10" diameter white paper plates*
- ☐ 5 7"-8" diameter yellow paper plates
- ☐ tracing paper
- ☐ hot glue gun and glue sticks
- ☐ pencil
- ☐ scissors

*Choose plates with ridged edges for a more realistic look.

To make one Daisy:

1. Set 1 white paper plate aside. Make photocopies of the petal and center A-E patterns, pages 19-20. **Note:** If you don't have access to a copier, you can trace the patterns onto tracing paper and cut out.

2. For each petal, place the rounded end on the ridged edge of a plate and draw around the pattern (you should be able to draw 3 petals on each plate); cut out.

3. For the center, draw around each pattern on a yellow plate; cut out. To fringe, cut 1" deep slits spaced about 1/8"-1/4" apart around the edges of each center circle. Use a pencil to curl under the fringed edges of each circle.

4. To add texture to the petals, fold and crease each petal in half lengthwise; unfold. Spacing the creases about 1/4"-1/2" apart continue to fold and crease the petals on either side of the center to the outer edges. Slightly curl the outer edges of each petal toward the center.

5. Imagine the remaining white paper plate as a clock face. Placing the pointed end about 1" inside the plate rim, glue a petal at each hour position around the clock (12 petals placed). With the remaining 12 petals, fill in the spaces between the outer petals.

6. Starting with E and ending with A, layer and glue the centers together. Glue the assembled center in the center of the petals.

Giant Daisy Patterns

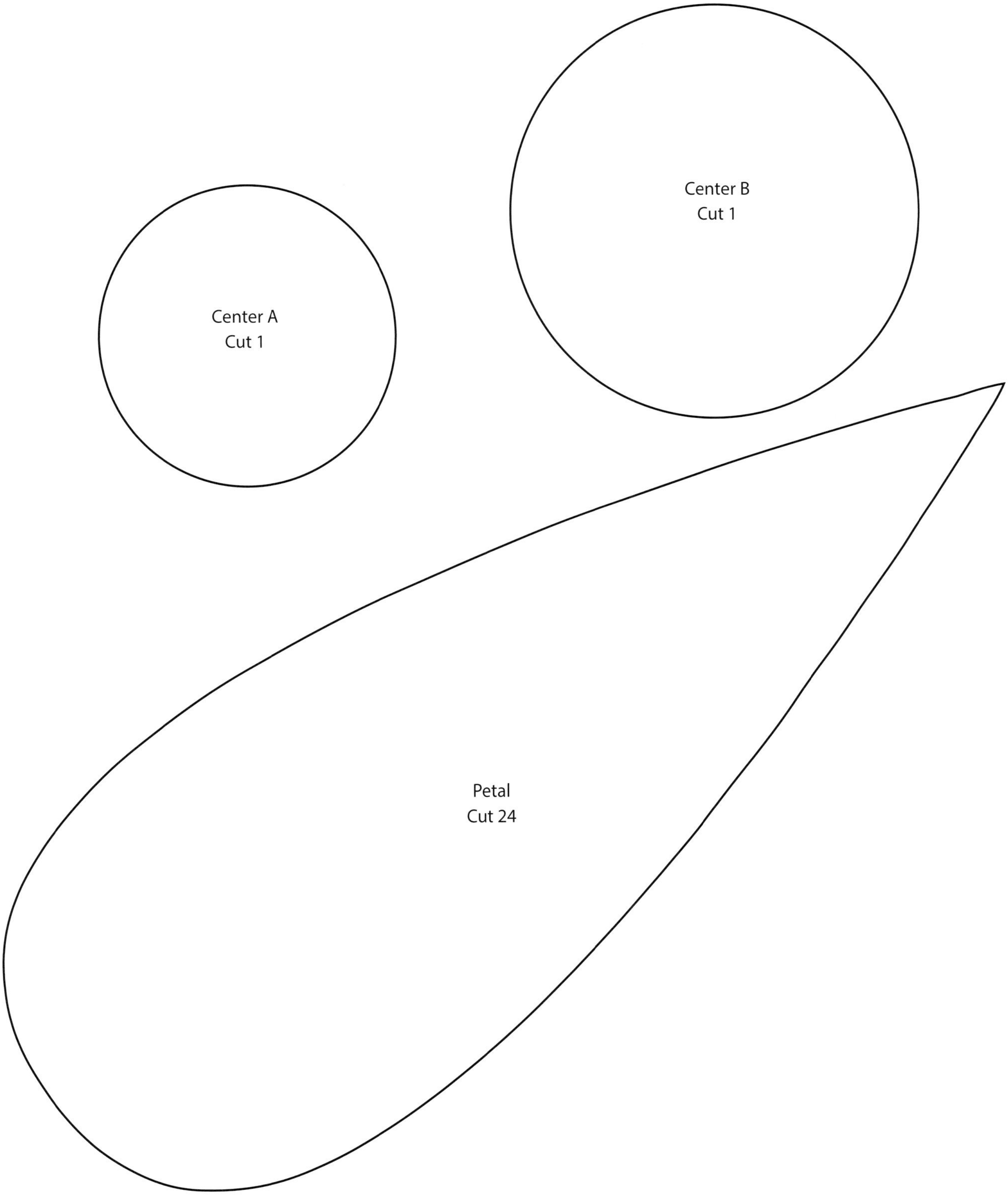

Leisure Arts Inc., grants the owner of this book permission to copy the patterns on this page for personal use only.

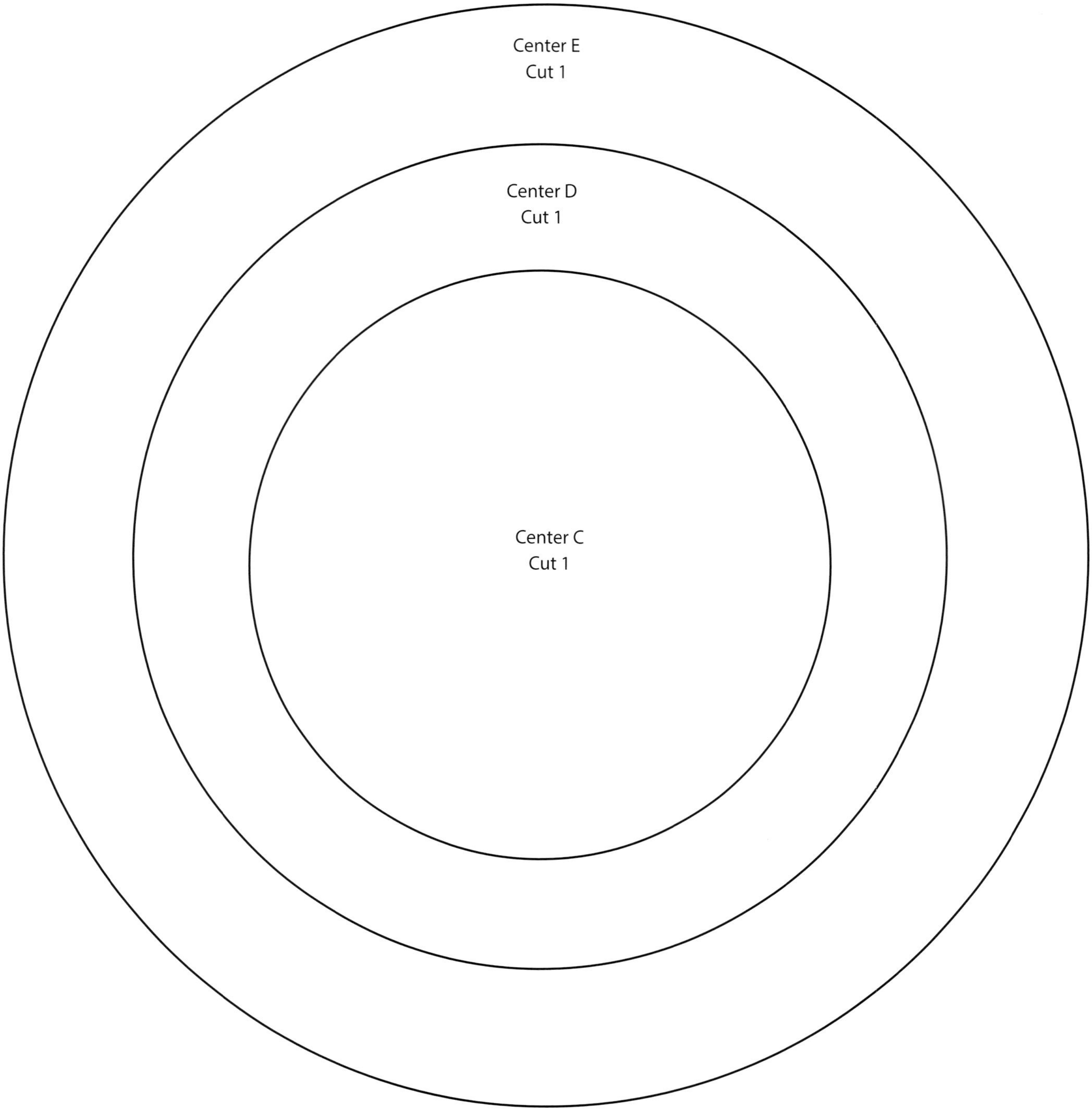
Center E
Cut 1
Center D
Cut 1
Center C
Cut 1

Rose

The Rose is one of the most beautiful paper flowers you can make. Using coffee filters for the petals gives the finished flower a very realistic look. A dozen Roses gathered together and tied with ribbon makes a gorgeous wedding bouquet.

Shopping List
(for 1flower)

- ☐ 8 white cone coffee filters
- ☐ green cloth-covered 20-gauge stem wire
- ☐ green floral tape
- ☐ red or pink liquid food coloring
- ☐ deep container of water
- ☐ spray water bottle with a fine mist setting
- ☐ chopstick or 1/8" diameter dowel
- ☐ hot glue gun and glue sticks
- ☐ pencil
- ☐ scissors

To make one Rose:

1. Open the coffee filters along the seam; flatten. Trace patterns A-H, pages 24-25, onto the filters the number of times indicated on each pattern; cut out just inside the drawn lines.

2. To make the center bud (petals A-C), apply a drop of glue to a stem about 1/2" from one end. Press one corner of the bottom edge of an A petal into the glue and wrap the petal tightly around the stem; Use floral tape to secure the end of the petal.

3. Beginning 1/4 turn from the end of the first petal and using floral tape to secure the bottom edge, wrap the remaining petal A tightly around the stem. Repeat to add the B and C petals.

4. To add the middle layer, begin just below the center bud with a petal D. Follow Step 3, wrapping a little less tightly. Add the remaining petal D 1/4 turn from the end of the previous petal.

5. To add the outer layers of petals (petals E-H), begin just below the middle petals and tape the pointed end of a petal E to opposite sides of the stem. Add the remaining E petals opposite the first two. Repeat to add petals F-H.

DIY Project Suggestion:
To make a bouquet, you will need a dozen Roses with stems at least 10" long. Holding the flowers by the stems, arrange four Roses into a circular shape. Just slightly below those blooms, add an outer ring of 8 Roses. Fluff and arrange the blooms unti you are pleased with the shape. Secure the stems with rubber bands, one just under the sepals and one near the end of the stems. Starting at the stem end and working toward the bloom and securing with glue as needed, wrap the stems with pink and white ribbons; knot just below the blooms and trim ribbon ends at an angle.

Tip: For extra stability, you may want to add a 10" length of dowel in center of the stems as you arrange the roses.

Finished Flower Size: approximately 4" diameter

6. To make the sepal, tightly wrap the base of the flower with floral tape several times.

7. To dye the flower, fill a bowl with water and add a few drops of food coloring. Test the color by dipping a piece of coffee filter into the dye. If the color is too dark, add water. If the color is too light add drops of food coloring, one at a time, until you reach the shade you desire. Dip the flower into the dye; remove and hang upside down to dry for an hour. **Note:** The dried flower color will be slightly lighter than when wet.

8. Wrap each petal tip around the chopstick or dowel to curl.

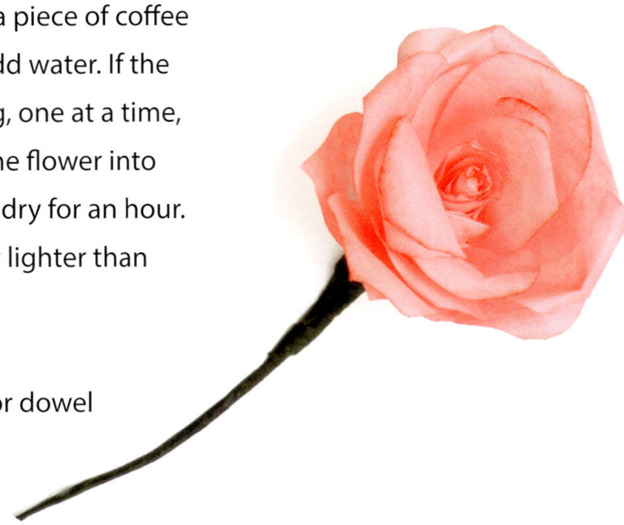

Rose Patterns

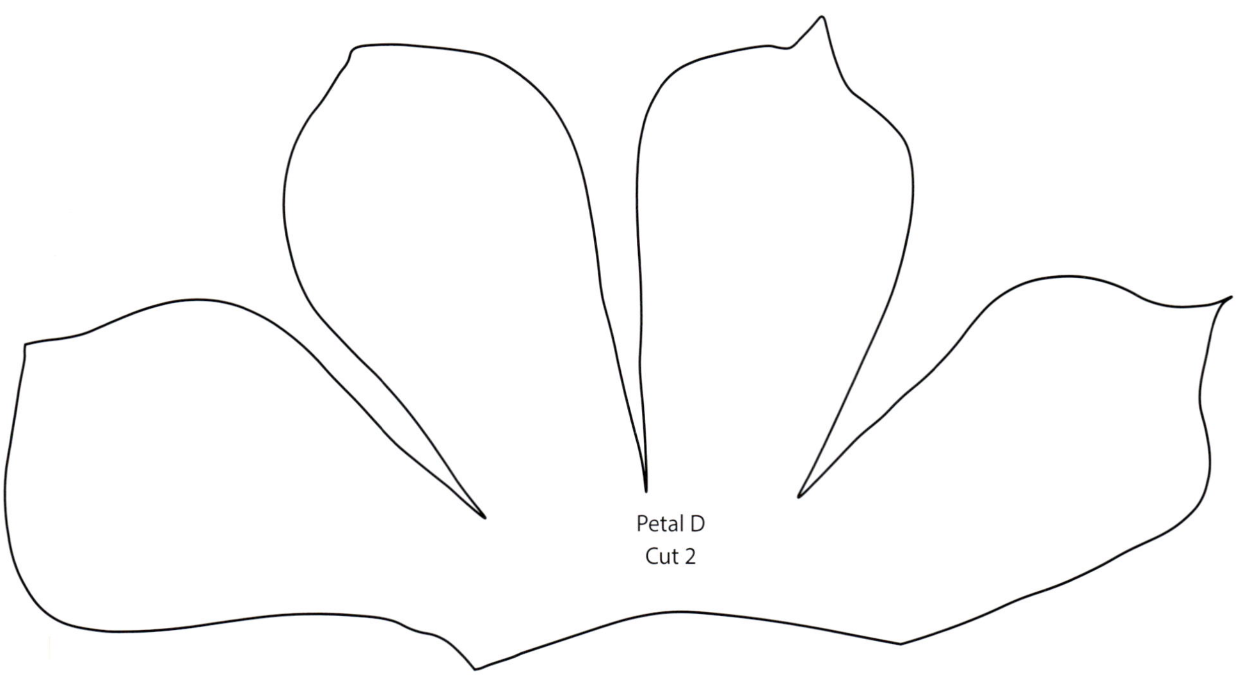

Leisure Arts Inc., grants the owner of this book permission to copy the patterns on pages 24 & 25 page for personal use only.

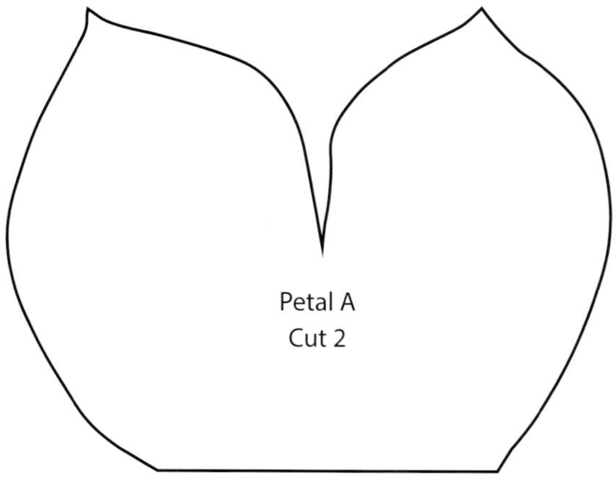
Petal A
Cut 2

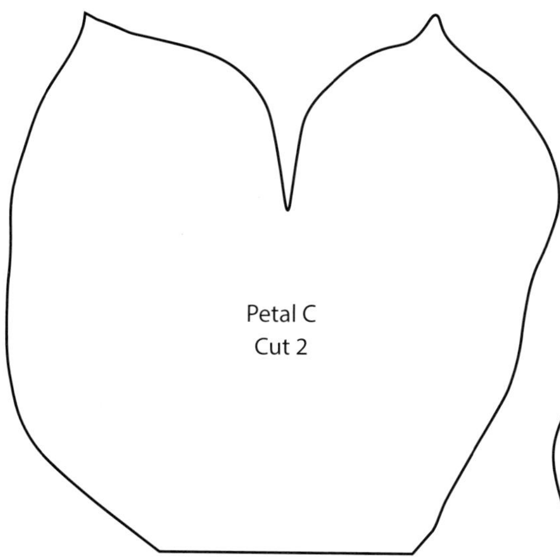
Petal C
Cut 2

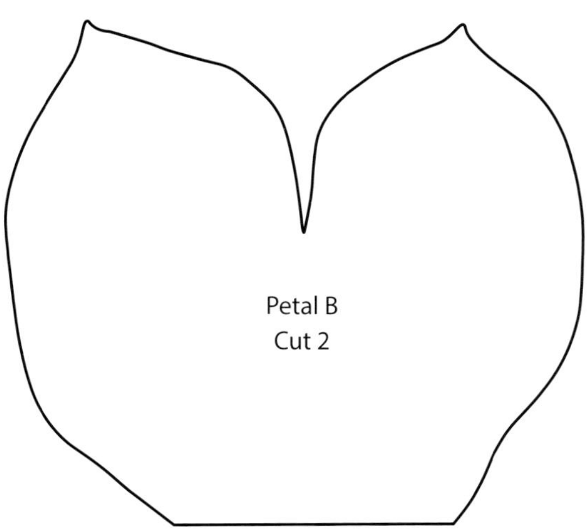
Petal B
Cut 2

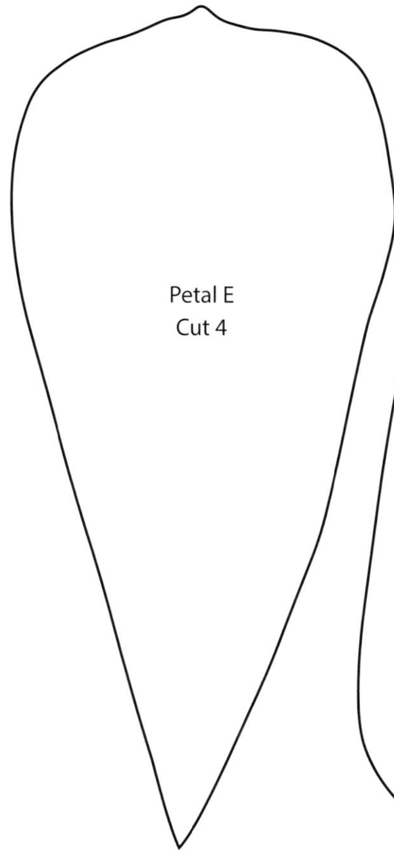
Petal E
Cut 4

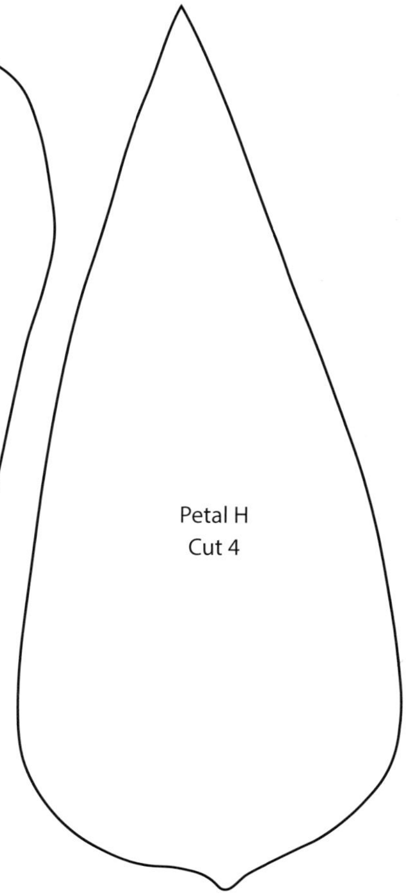
Petal H
Cut 4

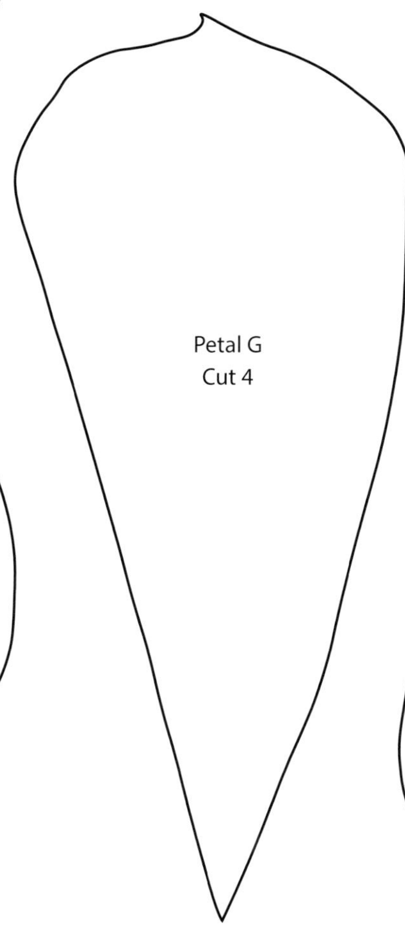
Petal G
Cut 4

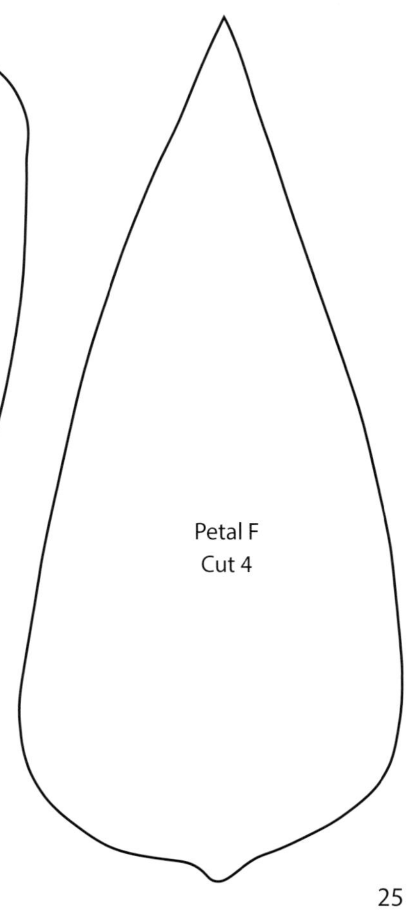
Petal F
Cut 4

Finished Flower Size: approximately 3" diameter

Poppy

Red Poppies are often worn on Memorial Day in remembrance of military members who have died in the service of their country. Poppies also come in shades of yellow, cream, orange, purple, and blue. These Poppies are made from cupcake liners to replicate the ruffled petals of the flower.

Shopping List

(for 1 flower)

- ☐ standard-size cupcake liners (red and purple)
- ☐ green cloth-covered 24-gauge stem wire
- ☐ green floral tape
- ☐ tracing paper (optional)
- ☐ craft glue
- ☐ pencil
- ☐ scissors

To make one Poppy:

1. Gently open and flatten 6 red liners and 1 purple liner. Make photocopies of the petal, center, and stamen patterns, page 29. **Note:** If you don't have access to a copier, you can trace the patterns on to tracing paper and cut out **or** if your cupcake liners are thin enough to see through, you can trace the patterns directly onto the liners. Use the patterns to cut out the number of pieces indicated on each pattern from the liners. Cut the 3 petals apart where indicated to make a total of 6 petals. Save the scraps.

2. To make the flower center, roll scraps into a tight 3/4" diameter ball. Insert a stem into the ball and secure with glue. With the wrong side facing up, place a thin line of glue close to the edge of the center. Wrap the center around the ball and stem, like a lollipop. Secure with more glue and floral tape as needed.

3. Make 1/2" deep cuts, spaced approximately 1/8" apart around the outer edge of the stamen. Wrap and glue the stamen around the base of the center.

4. Glue a petal under the center. Glue a second petal directly opposite the first one. Add 2 more petals at 60º angles on each side of the first petal. Filling in the open spaces between the petals, glue the last 2 petals to the center.

5. Cover the petal ends and create a sepal by wrapping the base of the flower and stem with floral tape, stopping about 1 1/2" below the flower.

DIY Project Suggestion:

This easy Poppy makes a great hair ornament and lasts much longer than a real flower. You can cut the stems to about 3" long and simply insert the stems into a bun or braid. To use on a comb, barrette, or clip, cut the stems close to the base of the flower and glue the blossom to the accessory.

Poppy Patterns

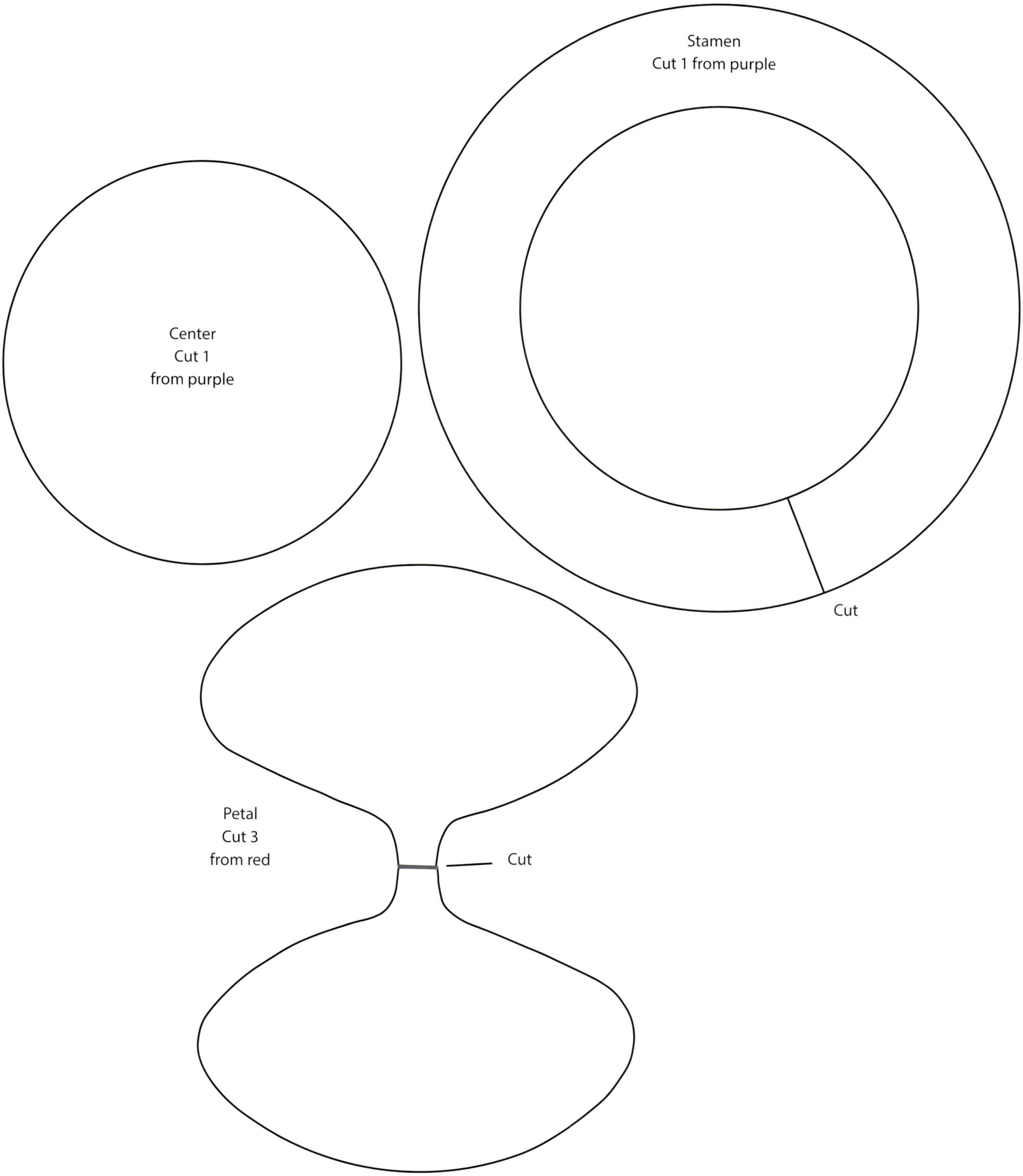

Leisure Arts Inc., grants the owner of this book permission to copy the patterns on this page for personal use only.

Finished Flower Size: approximately $1^1/_2$" diameter

Dandelion

Providing bright spots of color in lawns and pastures, the yellow flowers of the Dandelion are one of the first signs of spring. Real Dandelions have a short lifespan, but you can now enjoy this cheerful flower all year long when you make this paper version! When making the flower you can either cut out the pieces using a Cricut Maker™ or scissors.

Shopping List
(for 1 flower)

- ☐ 20 lb copier paper (yellow)
- ☐ lightweight cardstock (green)
- ☐ green cloth-covered 24-gauge stem wire (optional)
- ☐ tracing paper (optional)
- ☐ craft glue
- ☐ pencil
- ☐ scissors
- ☐ needle-nose pliers (optional)
- ☐ Cricut Maker™ (optional)

To make one Dandelion:

If using a Cricut Maker, begin with Step 1. If using scissors, begin with Step 2.

1. To download the SVG files for use with the Cricut Maker™ go to: bit.ly/7241_dandelion. If you need instructions on how to download SVG files, go to https://jennifermaker.com/paper-flowers-book. Once all the patterns are cut, skip to Step 3.

2. Make photocopies of the petal patterns A-B and sepal patterns C-D, page 33. **Note:** If you don't have access to a copier, you can trace the patterns onto tracing paper and cut out. Use the patterns to cut out the number of pieces indicated on each pattern from yellow paper for the petals or green cardstock for the sepals.

3. *With the end of the stem 1/2" below the top edge of the petal, glue one short straight edge of petal A to the end of a stem; allow glue to dry. Matching short ends, glue both petal B's and sepal C together to make one long strip. Glue the free end of B to the free end of A.

4. Tightly roll the petal/sepal strip around the stem to make a tight bud, gluing the end of C to the bud. Apply a liberal amount of glue to the underside of the bud to keep the rolled strips in place.

5. Starting at the outer edge and working toward the center, spread and fluff the sepal and petals until you are pleased with the shape of the flower.

6. Make a small hole in the center of sepal D. Apply glue to top side of the sepal between the hole and the points and slide the sepal up the stem to cover the bottom edges of the rolled strip. If any of the stem shows above the flower, use needle-nose pliers to bend the tip over about 1/4".

*If you are making your flowers to decorate a frame or other flat surface, do not glue A to a stem. Matching short edges, glue A, both B's, and C together to make one long s trip and then roll the strip into a tight bud; glue the end of C to the bud. Glue D to the bottom of the bud and fluff the petals.

DIY Project Suggestion:
Freshen up a metal chalkboard by gluing Dandelion blooms around the edges of the frame.

Dandelion Patterns

Leisure Arts Inc., grants the owner of this book permission to copy the patterns on this page for personal use only.

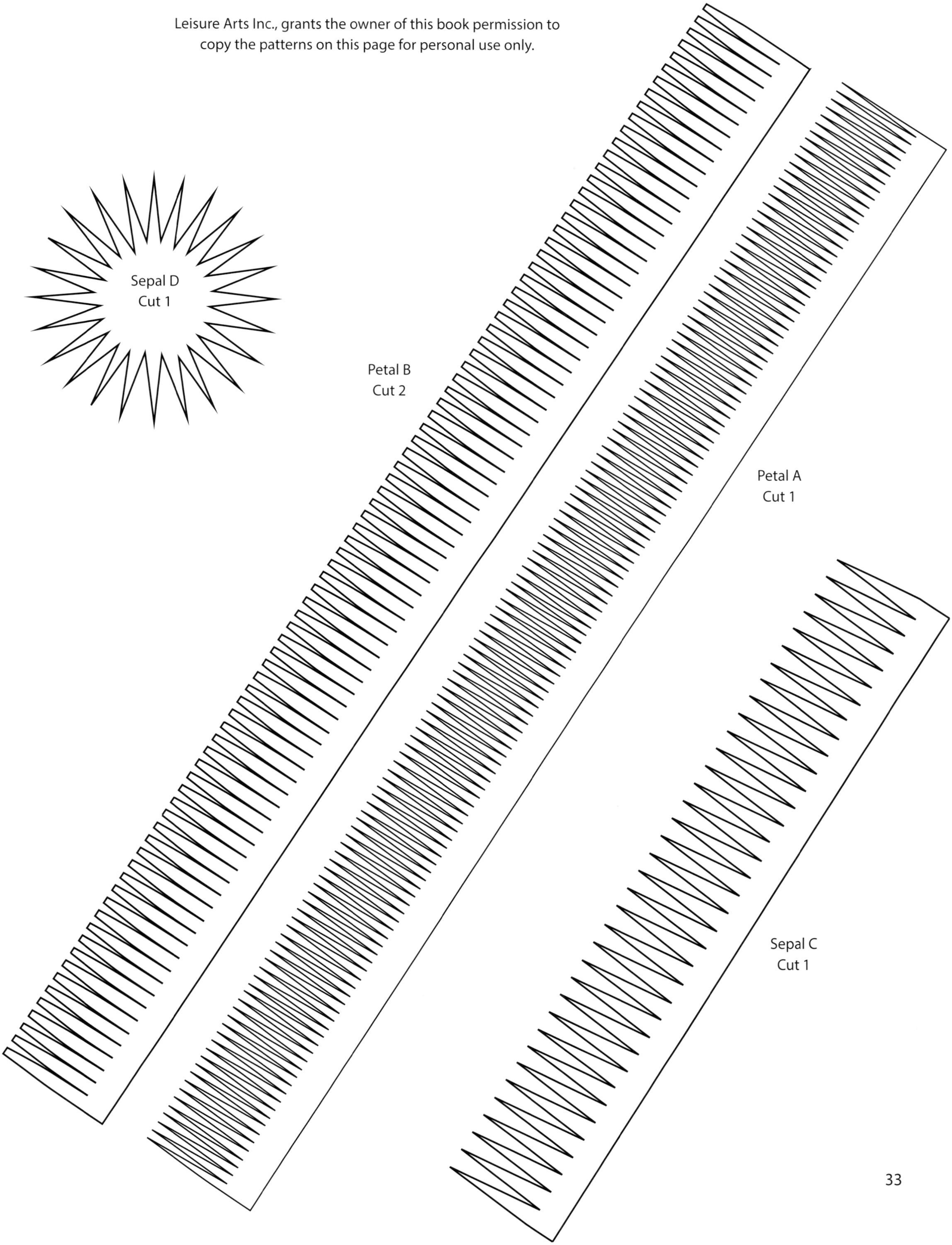

Finished Flower Size: approximately 5" diameter

Orchid

Orchids come in many varieties and colors, but my favorite is the Cattleya Orchid which is sometimes referred to as the corsage orchid. The petals in my orchid are cut from craft foam, pressed into a silicone flower impression mat to add texture, and accented with oil pastels which gives the flower a realistic look. When making the flower you can either cut out the pieces using a Cricut Maker™ or scissors.

Shopping List

(for 1 flower)

- ☐ white craft foam (1mm thick or less)
- ☐ 4" length of yellow chenille stem
- ☐ 24-gauge green floral stem
- ☐ 26-gauge silver floral wire
- ☐ green floral tape
- ☐ tracing paper (optional)
- ☐ soft oil pastels (purple and green)
- ☐ small sponge
- ☐ hot glue gun and glue sticks
- ☐ small candle
- ☐ craft glue
- ☐ scissors
- ☐ silicone flower impression mat* and an iron (optional)
- ☐ Cricut Maker™ (optional)

* silicone impression mats are located with the cake decorating supplies in craft stores

To make one Orchid:

Skip Step 3 if not using a silicone flower impression mat.

1. To download the SVG files for use with the Cricut Maker™ go to: bit.ly/7241_orchid. If you need instructions on how to download SVG files, go to https://jennifermaker.com/paper-flowers-book. Once all the patterns are cut, skip to Step 3.

2. Make photocopies of the petal, lip, and, sepal patterns. **Note:** If you don't have access to a copier, you can trace the patterns onto tracing paper; cut out. Use the patterns to cut out the number of pieces indicated on each pattern from craft foam.

3. If using a flower impression mat, set the iron to a medium temperature. Carefully hold the iron above, but not touching, a petal for about 5 seconds or until the foam starts to soften. Immediately press the petal firmly against the mat. Repeat with remaining petal, lip, and sepals.

4. Lightly color the front and back edges of each petal, lip, and sepal with the purple pastel. Use a dry sponge to blend and soften the color. At the base of each petal, lip, and sepal, use the green pastel to lightly color the center. Blend and soften the color with the sponge.

5. To ruffle the petal edges, hold a section of a petal edge 1"-2" above the candle flame for a few seconds until it softens, then quickly, but gently stretch the warm edge; repeat to ruffle the entire edge. Ruffle each petal, lip, and sepal edge.

6. For the stamen, fold the chenille stem in half and glue the ends to one end of a stem.

7. Place a line of glue along the bottom (straight) edge of the lip. Overlapping edges, wrap the lip around the stem, just below the stamen.

8. Cut five 5" lengths of floral wire. With one end about 1" above the bottom edge of the petal, glue a wire length to the center of a petal. Applying more glue if needed, pinch the petal center together to enclose the wire. Repeat for the remaining petal and the sepals.

9. Position the petals on opposite sides of the lip; attach the wires to the stem with floral tape. Position the sepals around the lip, between and just below the petals. Starting at the base of the flower and working down the stem, securely wrap the wires with floral tape.

Orchid Patterns

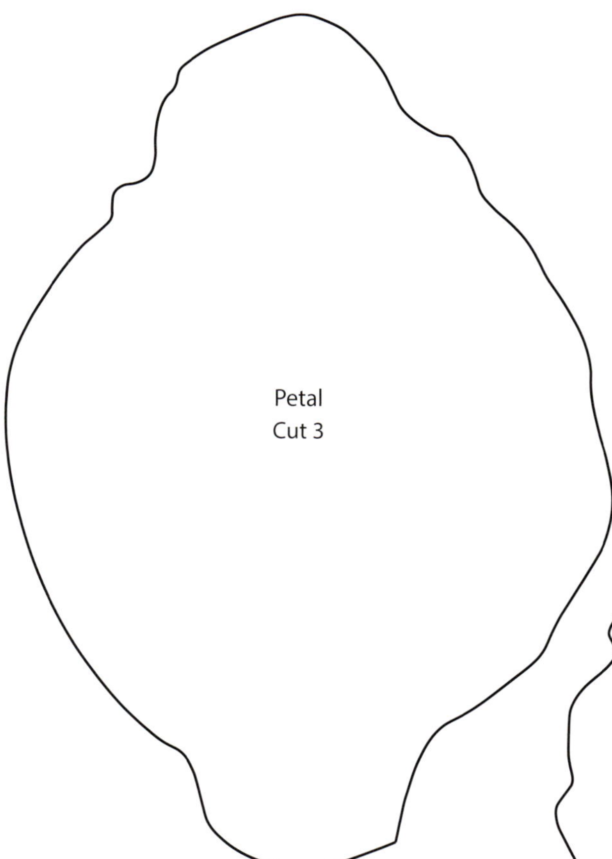

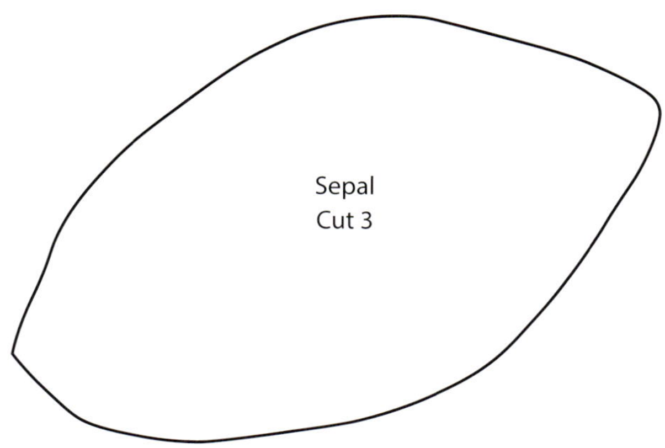

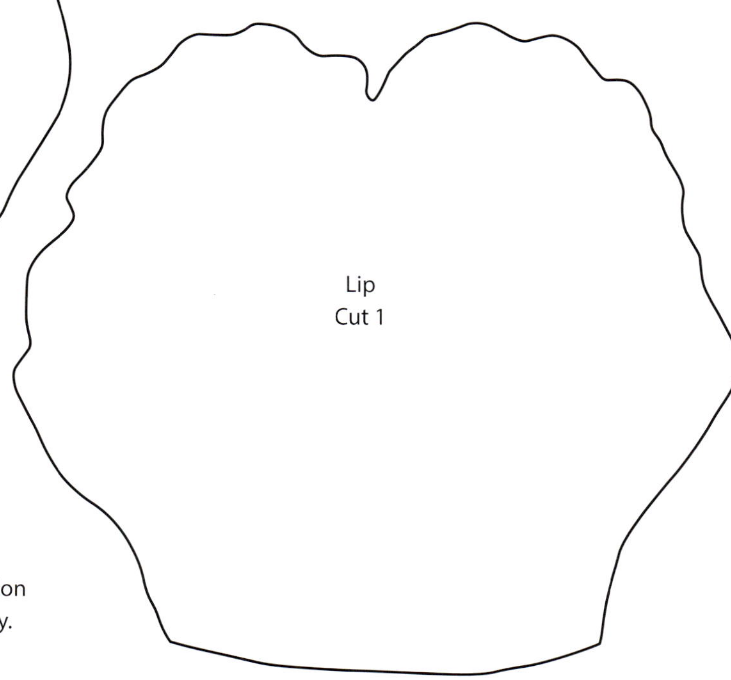

Leisure Arts Inc., grants the owner of this book permission to copy the patterns on this page for personal use only.

Finished Flower Size: approximately 24" diameter

Peony

The Peony has large, fragile petals and using tissue paper for the blooms replicates the look of the real flower. Peonies come in many colors including shades of red, pink, white, and purple. These flowers can be made with or without the yellow center. To use as a centerpiece, do not add the yellow center and place a tall glass candle holder in the center of each flower.

Shopping List
(for 1 flower)

- ☐ 20" x 26" red, white or pink tissue paper (12 sheets for each flower)
- ☐ 20" x 26" yellow tissue paper (4 sheets for each flower for flower center)
- ☐ 10" diameter sturdy paper plate or cardboard circle (1 for each flower)
- ☐ chenille stems (1 yellow and 4 of each flower color)
- ☐ lightweight copier paper
- ☐ hot glue and glue sticks
- ☐ pencil
- ☐ scissors

DIY Project Suggestion:

Delight your guests with a centerpiece of three brightly colored Peonies. Simply follow the instructions for making the flowers without centers. Place a tall glass votive in the center of each flower.

To make one Peony:

If making flowers with yellow centers, begin with Step 1. If making flowers without centers, begin with Step 6.

1. For the optional center, cut the 4 sheets of yellow paper in half lengthwise; stack the sheets.

2. Starting on one short end, fold the stack accordian style with 1" wide folds until the entire length is folded. Without compressing the paper, wrap a yellow chenille stem around the center of the folded paper.

3. Make a photocopy of the petal pattern **or** trace the petal pattern onto copier paper; cut out. Using the pattern as a guide, cut rounded tips on both ends of the folded paper.

4. One sheet at a time, gently pull the layers apart and toward the center to create a rounded shape.

5. Glue the flower center to the center of a paper plate.

6. For a petal section, stack 4 sheets of flower-color tissue paper. Starting on one short end, fold the stack accordian style with 1" wide folds until the entire length is folded.

7. Place a mark 11" from one end of the folded paper. Without compressing the paper, wrap a matching color chenille stem around the folded paper at the mark.

8. Using the petal pattern as a guide, cut rounded tips on both ends of the paper.

9. One sheet at a time, gently pull the layers apart and fluff. Because the chenile stem was placed off-center, the petals will be shorter on one side. After seperating each layer, pull the shorter petals toward the longer ones, hiding the chenile stem.

10. Repeat Steps 6-9 with remaining sheets of flower-color paper to make 2 more petal sections.

11. With the longer petals to the outside and the sections touching at the sides, glue the 3 petal sections to the plate perimeter around the yellow center (if using a center) or leaving the center open for a candle holder.

Peony Pattern

Leisure Arts Inc., grants the owner of this book permission to copy the patterns on this page for personal use only.

Finished Flower Size: approximately 12" diameter

Giant Tea Rose

The hybrid Tea Rose with its many layers of petals is one of the most beautiful varieties of roses. Tea Rose colors include, red, white, cream, peach, pink, and purple. When making this flower you can either cut out the pieces using a Cricut Maker™ or scissors.

Shopping List

(for 1 flower)

- ☐ 20 lb copier paper (salmon)
- ☐ lightweight cardstock (green)
- ☐ green floral tape
- ☐ 2 10"-12" long chopsticks or 1/4" diameter dowels
- ☐ spray water bottle with a fine mist setting
- ☐ tracing paper (optional)
- ☐ stylus (optional)
- ☐ hot glue gun and glue sticks
- ☐ pencil
- ☐ scissors
- ☐ Cricut Maker™ (optional)

To make one Tea Rose:

To use a Cricut Maker to cut, begin with Step 1. To use scissors to cut, begin with Step 2.

1. To download the SVG files for use with the Cricut Maker™ go to: bit.ly/7241_giant_tea_rose. If you need instructions on how to download SVG files, go to https://jennifermaker.com/paper-flowers-book. Once all the patterns are cut, skip to Step 3.

2. Make photocopies of the petal patterns A-I, sepal, and leaf, pages 46-47. **Note:** If you don't have access to a copier, you can trace the patterns on to tracing paper and cut out. Use the patterns to cut out the number of pieces indicated on each pattern from cardstock.

3. About 1" from one end, tightly wrap and glue an A petal around the end of a chopstick or dowel. This makes the center of the rose.

4. Beginning opposite the first petal and not wrapping quite as tightly, wrap and glue another A petal around the stem. Wrapping just a little looser each time, repeat to add the remaining two A petals at 90° angles from the first two petals. At this point you should have what looks like a tightly wound rosebud.

5. Lightly mist the tips of the petals B with water. Roll the petal tips around the chopstick or dowel to curl; allow to dry. Repeat with each group of petals C-I.

DIY Project Suggestion:
Use your Giant Tea Rose in place of a traditional bouquet for a wedding. To make the stem easier to hold, glue 2 additional lengths of dowel to the existing stem; wrap the entire stem with floral tape. To add an additional festive touch, wrap the stem with ribbon and tie the ends into a bow.

6. With the wraps slightly looser each time, follow Steps3-4 to add the four B petals.

7. Turn the flower over so the bottom is facing up. From this point on, when adding new petals you will be gluing them to the bottom of the existing ones instead of to the dowel.

8. Overlap and glue the bottom slits on a C petal to make the petals cup; repeat for each C petal. Glue two C petals on opposite sides of the flower; glue the remaining 2 petals at 90° angles from the first two.

9. Repeating Step 7 for each petal D-I, continue to add the petals to the flower.

Note: You can adjust the size of your Tea Rose by using fewer petals or adding additional petals. To add more petals, make additional photocopies of the largest petal pattern increasing the size by 20% each time.

10. Spacing equally around the bloom, glue the sepals to the bottom of the flower.

11. Fold each leaf in half lengthwise and crease to make a center vein; open the leaf. Use the point of a chopstick or a stylus to score diagonal veins, about 1/4" apart, from the center vein to the edges. Spacing at 90° angles, glue the leaves to the bottom of the flower.

12. Wrap the dowel with floral tape.

Giant Tea Rose Patterns

Leisure Arts Inc., grants the owner of this book permission to copy the patterns on pageSs 46 & 47 for personal use only.

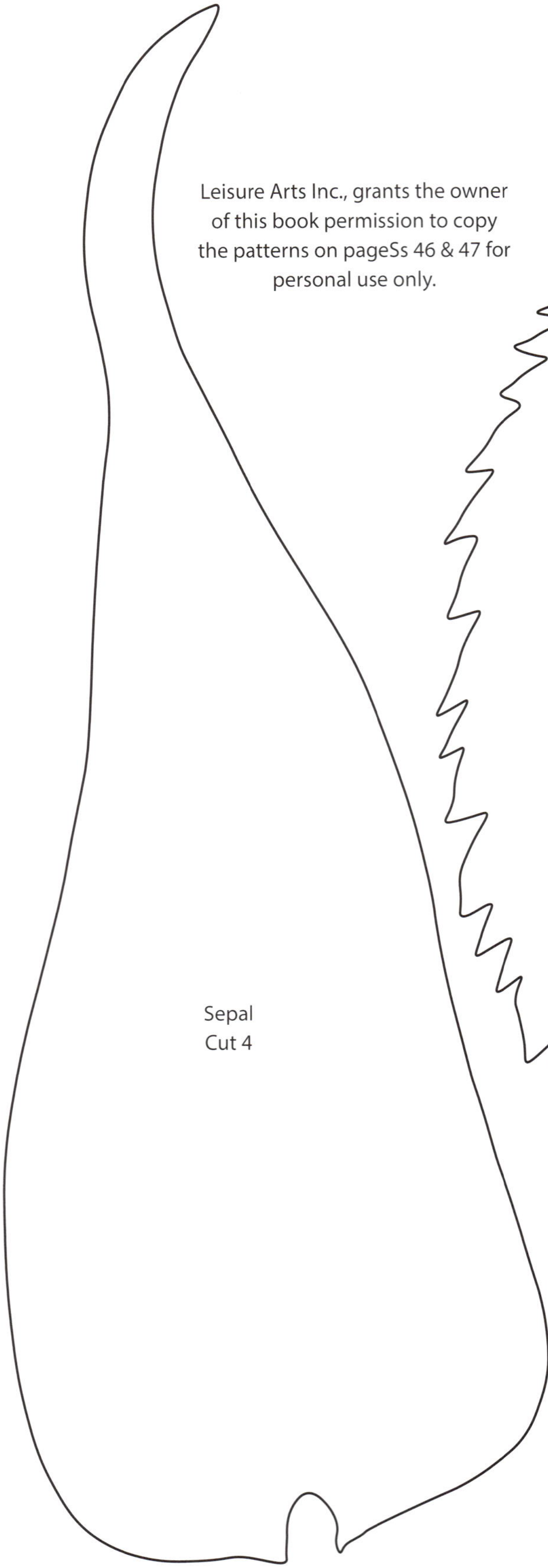

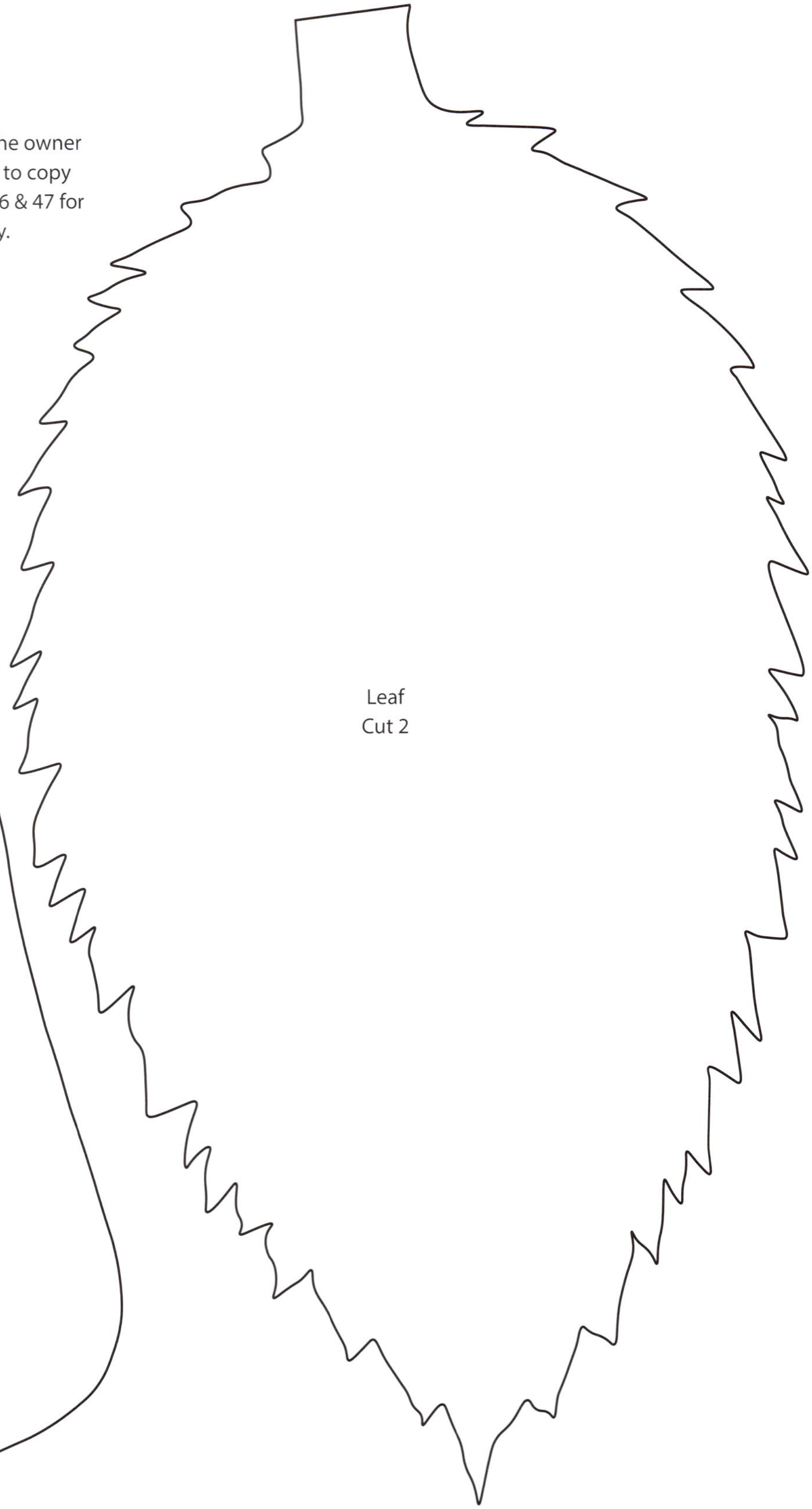

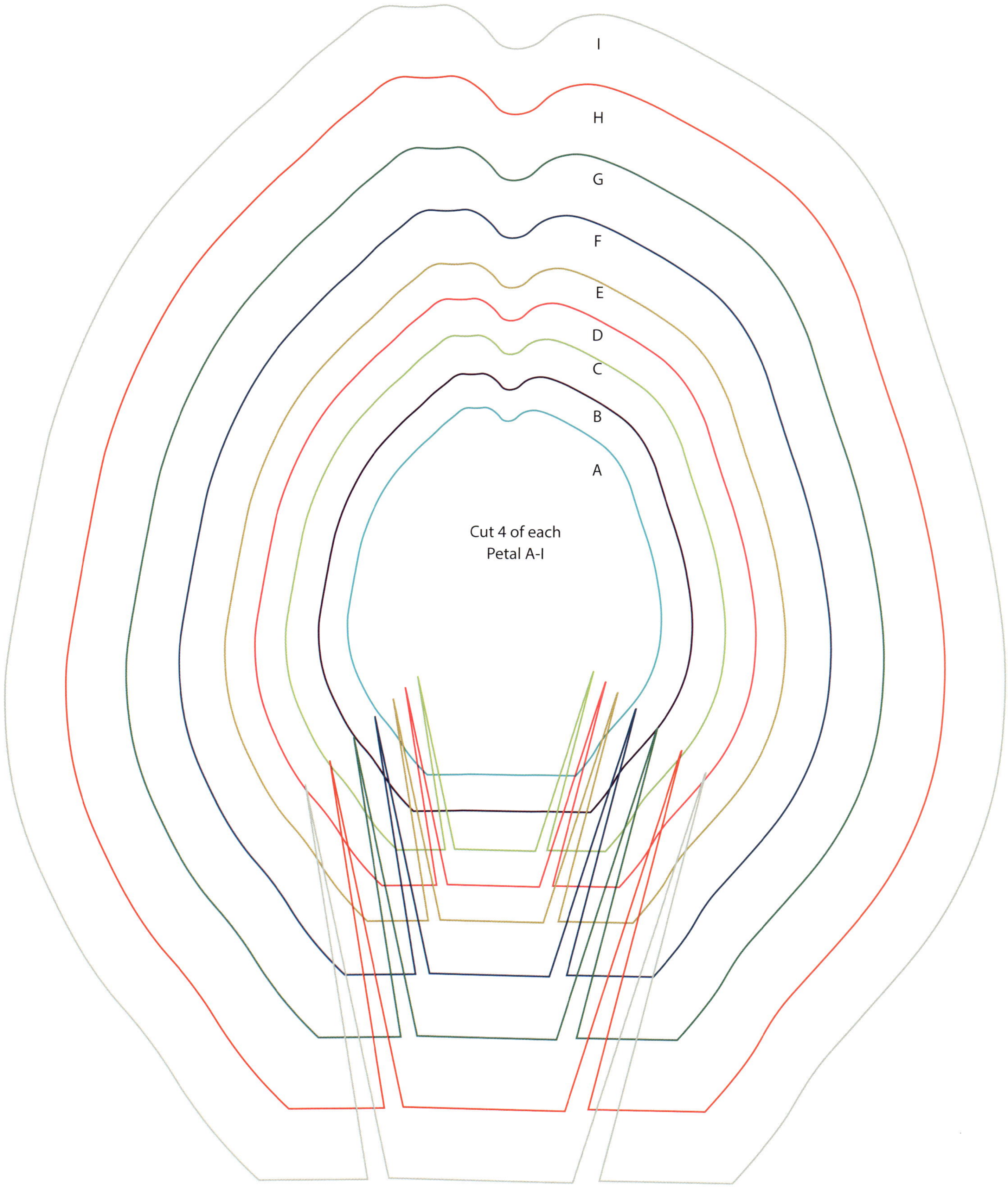
I
H
G
F
E
D
C
B
A
Cut 4 of each
Petal A-I

Meet Jennifer

Jennifer Maker is the artist name of Jennifer Marx, a "maker at heart" who draws more than 25,000 visitors a month to her web site devoted to crafts, DIY home decor, and food.

The Michigan-based mom and writer behind JenniferMaker.com has more than 20 years of experience as a graphic designer. The DIY project and craft blogger is also a bestselling travel author, historic fiber artist, and slightly eccentric upcycler.

"I love-love-love to create beautiful things, solve storage solutions, re-use and recycle old things, and save money," she says. "Every time I can showmy readers exactly how they, too, can have something so amazing of their own, my day is made."

Giant 3-D paper flowers are among her favorite projects. "They are so big and beautiful, and really stand out. I am a fan of realistic designs, and I find it a fun challenge to create something that looks true to the original."

Her other craft pursuits include 16th century costume design, historical smocking, blackwork embroidery, sweater upcycling, and hat making.

With her web site's step-by-step tutorials, she says, "I want to teach as many people as possible how to create beautiful things that bring happiness and creativity to their lives."

If you have questions about the SVG files in this book, please email hello@jennifermaker.com

To see some of my other designs, visit my blog at https://jennifermaker.com

Copyright © 2017 by Leisure Arts, Inc., 104 Champs Blvd., STE 100, Maumelle, AR 72113-6738, www.leisurearts.com. All rights reserved. This publication is protected under federal copyright laws. Reproduction or distribution of this publication or any other Leisure Arts publication, including publications which are out of print, is prohibited unless specifically authorized. This includes, but is not limited to, any form of reproduction or distribution on or through the Internet, including posting, scanning, or e-mail transmission.

We have made every effort to ensure that these instructions are accurate and complete. We cannot, however, be responsible for human error, typographical mistakes, or variations in individual work.

Production Team: Technical Writer – Jean Lewis; Technical Associate – Lisa Lancaster; Senior Graphic Artist – Lora Puls; Graphic Artist – Victoria Temple; Photostylist – Lori Wenger; Photographer – Jason Masters.